Postcards
from the
Planets

David Drew

2 January 2095

Dear Grandpa,
We blasted off from Earth last
night. You can see our space
bus in the sky just after take-
off. We're going to the Moon
first, and then the planets.
Will send you another postcard
soon.

Love, Kate

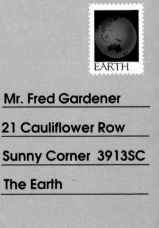

EARTH

Mr. Fred Gardener

21 Cauliflower Row

Sunny Corner 3913SC

The Earth

SPACE BUS AWAITS PERMISSION TO
DEPART EARTHPORT

3 January 2095

Dear Aunt Alice,
Here's what the Earth looks like
from our space bus. That's a
comet on the right. Dad and
Kate are feeling a bit
sick but I'm all right. Thanks
for promising to mind
my goldfish.
                    Love, Jessie.

P.S. Will post this on the Moon
tomorrow.

COMET HUGO PASSES CLOSE TO EARTH
ON ITS ORBIT AROUND THE SUN

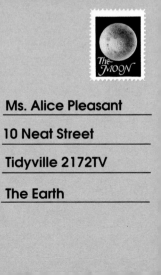

Ms. Alice Pleasant

10 Neat Street

Tidyville 2172TV

The Earth

12 January '95

Dear Aunt Alice,
Having a great time on the
Moon. There's no air, so the
stars don't twinkle. That's why
they look so clear through the
telescope. It's weird here. Even
when the Sun is shining the sky
is black. There's no blue sky
because there's no air.
            See you. Jessie.

The MOON

 Ms. Alice Pleasant

10 Neat Street

Tidyville 2172TV

The Earth

LUNAR INTERNATIONAL TELESCOPE
COMPLETED IN 2045

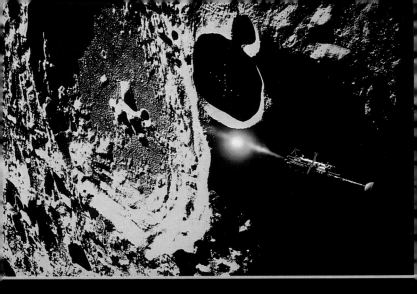

14 January

Dear Grandma,
We left the Moon last night. You
can see the base where we
stayed — it's inside a crater.
Jessie and I could jump really
high on the Moon because it
hasn't got much gravity.
I jumped higher than the
space bus.

           'Bye for now. Kate.

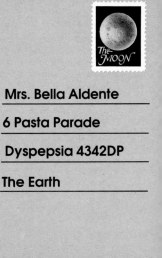

Mrs. Bella Aldente

6 Pasta Parade

Dyspepsia 4342DP

The Earth

LUNAR CENTRAL, THE MAIN TOURIST BASE
ON THE MOON, CATERS FOR 600 VISITORS.

21 January 2095

Dear Aunt Alice,
We touched down on Venus
this morning. Kate thought
there'd be Venus fly traps
everywhere. I told her she'd
have to be lucky because the
temperature is hot enough to
fry you. So we stayed inside our
landing capsule. The weather is
terrible — it rains acid most of
the time. From Venus orbit
the Earth looks like a bright star.
                Missing you. Jessie.

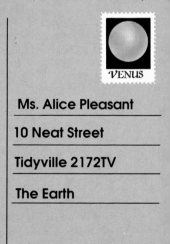

VENUS

Ms. Alice Pleasant

10 Neat Street

Tidyville 2172TV

The Earth

VENUS WITH THE VENUS LANDER IN ORBIT

1 Feb. '95

Dear Uncle Bert,
They've moved us into this
special spacecraft that resists
heat. Every day we get nearer
the Sun and even inside the
ship it's starting to warm up.
Flew past Mercury today. It's
the planet nearest the Sun.
If you were on Mercury you
would be roasted alive.
                    Love from Kate.

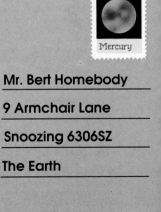

Mercury

Mr. Bert Homebody

9 Armchair Lane

Snoozing 6306SZ

The Earth

SUNSHIP PASSING MERCURY AS IT TAKES
VISITORS ON THE SPECTACULAR
SOLAR FLYPAST

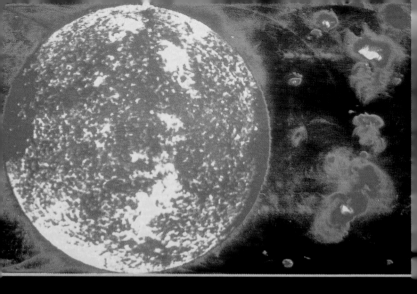

5 February 2095

Dear Grandpa,
We flew near the Sun today, but
no one was allowed to look at it
because the light can blind you.
A special camera took this
picture. The Sun is hotter in the
yellow part than it is in the red
parts called sunspots.
                    Love, Jessie.

Mr. Fred Gardener

21 Cauliflower Row

Sunny Corner 3913SC

The Earth

SUNSPOTS
(INFRARED PHOTOGRAPH)

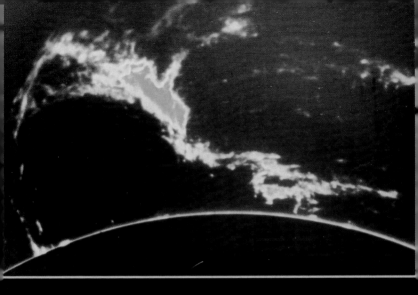

6 Feb.

Dear Grandma,
Here's a close-up picture of a
solar flare. It's as long as ten
Earths placed side by side.
These flares are made of hot,
glowing gases and they're
caused by huge explosions on
the surface of the Sun.
     Now we're leaving the
Sun behind us and heading for
the outer planets.
                    'Bye. Kate.

THE
SUN

Mrs. Bella Aldente

6 Pasta Parade

Dyspepsia 4342DP

The Earth

SOLAR FLARE

Friday, 27 February.

Dear Aunt Alice,
Reached the space station orbiting Mars on Tuesday. We hope to go down to the surface tomorrow. It looks hot down there but they say it's freezing. We went on an excursion to one of the moons yesterday. It was like a giant rock floating in space.

Are you remembering to feed my goldfish?

Jessie.

MARS AND PHOBOS:
PHOBOS IS A MOON ABOUT THE SIZE OF THE
CITY OF LONDON OR NEW YORK

MARS

Ms. Alice Pleasant

10 Neat Street

Tidyville 2172TV

The Earth

29 Feb.

Dear Uncle Bert,
Wow, you'd love this planet!
There is a volcano called
Olympus Mons that is higher than
Mount Everest. The valley we're
in is bigger than the Grand
Canyon. —Kate.

Dear Uncle,
I hate it here. The dust makes
me sneeze and there are no
animals or plants. People have
left litter all around the base.
It's a mess.   —Jessie.

THE FIRST BASE ON MARS HAS BEEN PRESERVED
AS A HISTORIC SITE. VISITORS ARE TRANS-
PORTED FROM MARS CITY BY HOVERPLANE.

MARS

Mr. Bert Homebody

9 Armchair Lane

Snoozing 6306SZ

The Earth

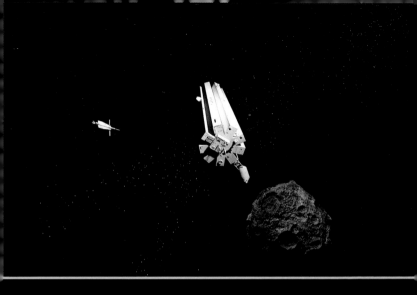

19 March 2095

Dear Aunt May,
It feels like we've been travelling
for ages. Every day the Sun looks
smaller because we're moving
away from it. We're passing the
asteroids which are just a lot of
old rocks. Kate saw a big space
ship drilling an asteroid for
minerals. I'm bored. Hope we
get to Jupiter soon. —Jessie.

P.S. Dad has taken up jogging
around inside the space bus. We
all do some exercise each day.

ASTEROID MINING

Asteroids

Ms. May Castoff

3 Purl Street

Knittington 5415KT

The Earth

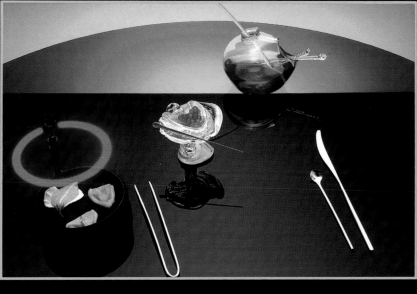

20 March

Dear Aunt Alice,
This space-ship food has to be
seen to be believed! It looks
like real meat and fruit but it's
all made out of chemicals.
And the drinks are great. —Kate.

I'd swap this stuff for real food
any day. It tastes like
cardboard. —Jessie.

SPACE FOOD: SUBSTITUTE MEAT,
ARTIFICIAL BLUEBERRIES AND
RECONSTITUTED FRUIT JUICE.

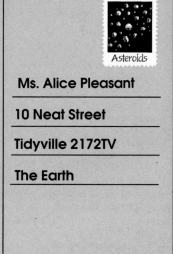

Asteroids

Ms. Alice Pleasant

10 Neat Street

Tidyville 2172TV

The Earth

28 March '95

Dear Grandma,
We've reached Jupiter at last.
From here the Sun looks no
bigger than a bright star. One of
Jupiter's moons is half as big as
the Earth. Jupiter is covered in
clouds and sometimes you can
see lightning. Love from Jessie.

P.S. I'd give anything for some
real food. (Such as one of your
double-decker spaghetti
sandwiches.)

JUPITER (THE LARGEST PLANET) AND
GANYMEDE (THE LARGEST MOON)

JUPITER

Mrs. Bella Aldente

6 Pasta Parade

Dyspepsia 4342DP

The Earth

29 March

Hi Grandpa.
Today we went hunting for
moons. Jupiter has sixteen of
them. The moon in the picture
is so close to Jupiter it sometimes touches the clouds. We
also saw a bigger moon called
Io (you pronounce it ee-o).
It looks like a pizza and
has volcanoes on it. — K.

Our next planet is Saturn, the
one with the beautiful rings.
It's the one I like best.   — J.

JUPITER

Mr. Fred Gardener

21 Cauliflower Row

Sunny Corner 3913SC

The Earth

MOONHUNTING AROUND JUPITER

11 April 2095

Dear Aunt Alice,
We're getting nearer to Saturn.
Today we flew past one of its
moons called Titan. Kate says
you could fit the Earth inside
Saturn 750 times. Although it's
big, Saturn is so light it would
float in water. We'll be flying
through the rings tomorrow.
Dad's a bit nervous we might
crash.   —Love, Jessie.

SATURN AND ITS MOONS. THIS VIEW, TAKEN
NEAR TITAN, MAKES TITAN LOOK MUCH
LARGER THAN IT IS.

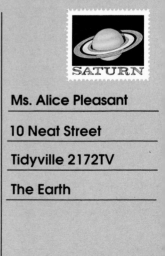

SATURN

Ms. Alice Pleasant

10 Neat Street

Tidyville 2172TV

The Earth

14 April 2095

Dear Uncle Bert,
This is what Saturn's rings looked
like when we passed through
them. The rings are made of
dust and rocks covered with ice.
There are spaces between the
rings wide enough for our space
bus to fit through.

    Now we have to triple our
speed because the next planet
is so far away.

                 —Kate.

SATURN

Mr. Bert Homebody

9 Armchair Lane

Snoozing 6306SZ

The Earth

SATURN'S RINGS, SEEN EDGE-ON

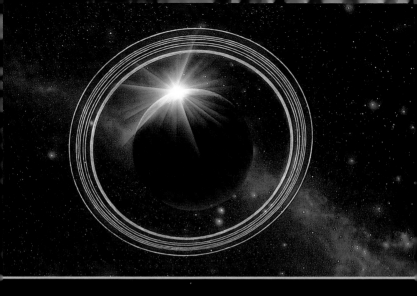

6 / 6 / 95

Dear Aunt Alice,
Did you know Uranus has rings,
too? When we passed behind
this planet we saw the Sun
shining from the other side. At
Uranus's south pole a single
night can last twenty years.
    It's awfully dark out here.
I think I'm ready to come home.
Wish you were here ... Jessie.

P.S. How's my goldfish?

URANUS

Ms. Alice Pleasant

10 Neat Street

Tidyville 2172TV

The Earth

THE RINGS OF URANUS

17 June 2095

Dear Grandpa,
Spent a few hours on one of
Uranus's moons, called Ariel.
Even when the Sun is shining
there's hardly any light out here.
We haven't seen a living thing
since we left Earth. Thanks for
the books you sent me. There's
not a lot to do here except
collect rocks. I've collected 93
so far.   — Kate.

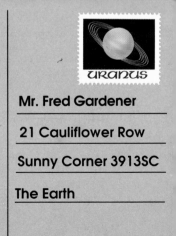

URANUS

Mr. Fred Gardener

21 Cauliflower Row

Sunny Corner 3913SC

The Earth

URANUS FROM ARIEL

11 July

Dear Aunt May,
We've been in orbit around
Neptune for a week now. It's a
pity these big planets are mostly
made of gas and liquid, because
it means we can't land on them.
But we spent a day on one of
Neptune's moons, called Triton.
Even when I dropped a big rock
I couldn't hear the crash. This
was because there was no air
to carry the sound.
                              Love from Jessie.

P.S. Thanks for the leg warmers.
It's really freezing out here,
even in our space suits.

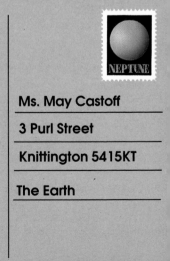

NEPTUNE

Ms. May Castoff

3 Purl Street

Knittington 5415KT

The Earth

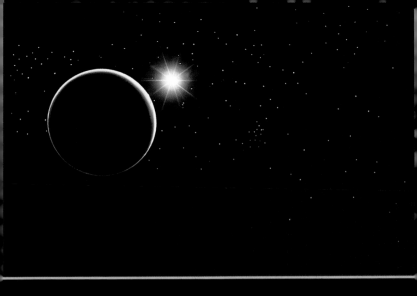

1 August

Dear Grandma,
This is Pluto. It's made of rock
and it's pretty boring. Some
people say there's a tenth
planet further out called
Planet X. We're going to look for
it, but I don't like our chances.
Anyway, I'd rather be heading
for home. I feel homesick. Jessie
feels the same. She says she
dreams every night about
eating real food, especially
spaghetti.   —Kate.

Mrs. Bella Aldente

6 Pasta Parade

Dyspepsia 4342DP

The Earth

PLUTO'S DARK SIDE

12 August

Dear Grandpa,
We didn't find the tenth planet
but there are a lot of comets
out here. They just seem to be
lumps of rock and ice, without
the long tails they get when
they fly past the Sun.

In a few months we'll be on
Earth again, probably by
New Year. We take the sleeping
drink tonight and when we
wake up we'll be almost home.
It's strange to think we'll be
asleep for four months. —Jessie.

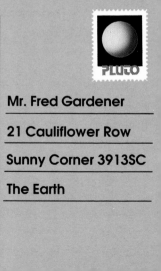

Mr. Fred Gardener

21 Cauliflower Row

Sunny Corner 3913SC

The Earth

COMET AXEL IN DEEP SPACE

"Is that you, Aunt May? ...
It's great to hear your voice again!
When I woke up we were already
in Earth orbit and now we can see
the space port just below us.
See you at home tomorrow!"

The Daily News

31 December 2095

Tourists arrive home by air taxi after their safe return to Earthport yesterday.

SPACE BUS RETURNS SAFELY

Earthport, Monday. — The space ship "Icarus" returned to Earth safely today after twelve months in space. Nicknamed the "space bus", the vehicle travelled to all nine planets in the Solar System.

The 86 crew and 405 passengers are reported in good health on their return.

The captain of the

"Icarus", Lieut. Wendy Coolhead, said on arrival that she experienced no in-flight difficulties apart from a girl who was caught raiding the ship's supplies in search of a spaghetti sandwich.